Jah Ra

Prayers

22 KING SELASSIE I & EMPRESS MENEN PRAYERS, WITH HEALING BIBLE PSALMS

By

Empress Yuajah

Life as a Rasta Woman

LIFE AS A
RASTA WOMAN

RASTA WAY
OF LIFE

RASTAFARI
LIVITY BOOK

EMPRESS
YUAJAH

How to Become a Rasta

How to Date

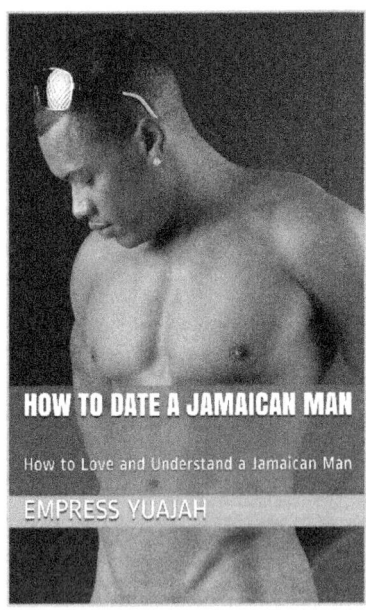

HOW TO DATE A JAMAICAN MAN

How to Love and Understand a Jamaican Man

EMPRESS YUAJAH

a Jamaican Man

Rasta Rules

Empress ♪ Rasta Rules

*144 Rastafarian Rules,
Laws and Regulations*

Conquering Lion of Judah, King Selassie I

Powerful Rasta Prayers

For those who seek to live a spiritual life in
Jah Rastafari.
Blessed Love.

The Rasta prayers are intended to <u>activate the powers of the Most High</u>, to help one find help and healing during a time of distress, need or comfort. The names of "King Selassie I," "Empress Menen" and "Jah" are the equivalent of saying "Jesus Christ" and "God" in Christianity. These names are used to invoke high, clean, positive constructive, spiritual energy.

The Bible Psalms

Read the Psalms scripture that follow each prayer, to help further activate and communicate your need, to Jah Rastafari for help, protection, healing, and strength.

ACKNOWLEDGMENTS

To the Almighty Creator. You love me and forgive me, always. Your mercy is as big as your Majesty. In you I put all my faith and all my trust, you are there for me even before I need you.
I and I give thanks. Jah Rastafari.

Table of Contents

The name of King Selassie I

In Rastafari the name "King Selassie I" is "Magical." If you believe in him and have a good heart, you will see results from your prayers.

The name of Empress Mennen
In Rastafari the name "Empress Menen." Is also "Magical." She has great relationships with women of Rastafari Livity. If you have a good heart, and prayer to Empress Menen, she will respond.

The Star of David

Rastafari is the oldest "Religion." Rastafari is "the Nazirite" vow of the Bible. The Star of David is often used to represent Rastafari and its ancient Davidic and Nazirite roots. Many of the psalms were written by King David himself as he communicated his heart to Jah.

King David, King Solomon, King Menelik I, King Menelik II and King Selassie I are all of the same Lineage. I wanted to include the energy of the Kings of the tribe of Judah, by including *the Star of David* as we read our Jah Rastafari Prayers and Psalms.

Jah Rastafari.

JAH RASTAFARI
MORNING PRAYER

Good Morning Jah, in the name of His Imperial Majesty, Holy Emanuel I, King Selassie I.

I and I give thanks for this blessed day.
May all the land be touched by your presence beauty and power.
Keep I and I protected from Babylon tricks and adversity.

Give I and I strength to survive another Day in Babylon.

Bless I and I that I may maintain a positive loving caring and sharing spirit as I serve you Jah on this day.

Keep Satan and his workers out of I and I path as I trod the earth today.

In the name of King Selassie I, Holy Emanuel I.
Rastafari.

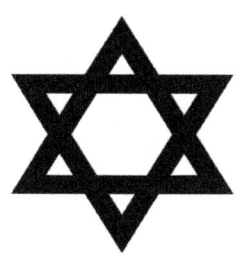

Bless the LORD, O my soul;
And all that is within me, bless His holy
name!
Bless the LORD, O my soul,
And forget not all His benefits:
Who forgives all your iniquities,
Who heals all your diseases,
Who redeems your life from destruction,
Who crowns you with loving-kindness and
tender mercies,
Who satisfies your mouth with good
things,
So that your youth is renewed like the
eagle's.

The LORD executes righteousness
and justice for all who are oppressed.

He made known His ways to Moses,
His acts to the children of Israel.

The LORD is merciful and gracious,
Slow to anger, and abounding in mercy.
He will not always strive with us,
nor will He keep His anger forever.
He has not dealt with us according to our
sins,
nor punished us according to our iniquities.

For as the heavens are high above the
earth,
So great is His mercy toward those who
fear Him;
As far as the east is from the west,
So far has He removed our transgressions
from us.
As a father pities his children,
so the LORD pities those who fear Him.
For He knows our frame;
He remembers that we are dust.

As for man, his days are like grass;
as a flower of the field, so he flourishes.
For the wind passes over it, and it is gone,
And its place remembers it no more.
But the mercy of the LORD is from
everlasting to everlasting
on those who fear Him,

And His righteousness to children's
children,
to such as keep His covenant,
And to those who remember His
commandments to do them.

The LORD has established His throne in
heaven,
and His kingdom rules over all.

Bless the LORD, you His angels,
Who excel in strength, who do His word,
Heeding the voice of His word.
Bless the LORD, all you His hosts,
You ministers of His, who do His pleasure.
Bless the LORD, all His works,
In all places of His dominion.

Bless the Lord, O my soul!

JAH RASTAFARI PRAYER
BEFORE EATING FOOD

Jah, I give thanks for this food. Bless this food Most High, that I and I am about to eat. May it nourish I temple, and give I strength.
In the name of the Most High,
I and I give thanks.
Jah Rastafari.

Blessed *is* every one that feareth the LORD; that walketh in his ways.

For thou shalt eat the labour of thine hands: happy *shalt* thou *be*, and *it shall be* well with thee.

Thy wife *shall be* as a fruitful vine by the sides of thine house: thy children like olive plants round about thy table.

Behold, that thus shall the man be blessed that feareth the LORD.

The LORD shall bless thee out of Zion: and thou shalt see the good of Jerusalem all the days of thy life.

Yea, thou shalt see thy children's children, *and* peace upon Israel.

JAH RASTAFARI PRAYER
FOR PROSPERITY

Jah, Jah, Jah. I know that your name said daily provides blessings.
I will say your name abundantly. Before and after I eat. When I wake up in the morning. Before I retire to sleep, please direct I and I path, and fill I and I heart, that I may serve you, and be blessed wealth and abundance. In King Selassie I name, Jah Rastafari.

Say the following Psalm out loud 1x in the morning before you begin any activities and 1x in the evening before sleeping.

I love you, Lord, my strength.
The Lord is my rock, my fortress and my
deliverer;
my God is my rock, in whom I take
refuge,
my shield and the horn of my salvation,
my stronghold.
I called to the Lord, who is worthy of
praise,
and I have been saved from my enemies.
The cords of death entangled me;
the cords of the grave coiled around me;
the snares of death confronted me.
In my distress I called to the Lord;
I cried to my God for help.
From his temple he heard my voice;
my cry came before him, into his ears.
The earth trembled and quaked,

and the foundations of the mountains
shook;
they trembled because he was angry.
Smoke rose from his nostrils;
consuming fire came from his mouth,
burning coals blazed out of it.
He parted the heavens and came down;
dark clouds were under his feet.
He mounted the cherubim and flew;
he soared on the wings of the wind.
He made darkness his covering, his
canopy around him—
the dark rain clouds of the sky.
Out of the brightness of his presence
clouds advanced,
with hailstones and bolts of lightning.
The Lord thundered from heaven;
the voice of the Most High resounded.
He shot his arrows and scattered the
enemy,
with great bolts of lightning he routed
them.
The valleys of the sea were exposed
and the foundations of the earth laid
bare
at your rebuke, Lord,
at the blast of breath from your nostrils.
He reached down from on high and took
hold of me;

he drew me out of deep waters.
He rescued me from my powerful enemy,
from my foes, who were too strong for
me.
They confronted me in the day of my
disaster,
but the Lord was my support.
He brought me out into a spacious place;
he rescued me because he delighted in
me.
The Lord has dealt with me according to
my righteousness;
according to the cleanness of my hands
he has rewarded me.
For I have kept the ways of the Lord;
I am not guilty of turning from my God.
All his laws are before me;
I have not turned away from his decrees.
I have been blameless before him
and have kept myself from sin.
The Lord has rewarded me according to
my righteousness,
according to the cleanness of my hands
in his sight.
To the faithful you show yourself faithful,
to the blameless you show yourself
blameless,
to the pure you show yourself pure,

but to the devious you show yourself shrewd.
You save the humble
but bring low those whose eyes are haughty.
You, Lord, keep my lamp burning;
my God turns my darkness into light.
With your help I can advance against a troop
with my God I can scale a wall.
As for God, his way is perfect:
The Lord's word is flawless;
he shields all who take refuge in him.
For who is God besides the Lord?
And who is the Rock except our God?
It is God who arms me with strength
and keeps my way secure.
He makes my feet like the feet of a deer;
he causes me to stand on the heights.
He trains my hands for battle;
my arms can bend a bow of bronze.
You make your saving help my shield,
and your right hand sustains me;
your help has made me great.
You provide a broad path for my feet,
so that my ankles do not give way.
I pursued my enemies and overtook them;
I did not turn back till they were

destroyed.
I crushed them so that they could not rise;
they fell beneath my feet.
You armed me with strength for battle;
you humbled my adversaries before me.
You made my enemies turn their backs in
flight,
and I destroyed my foes.
They cried for help, but there was no one
to save them—
to the Lord, but he did not answer.
I beat them as fine as windblown dust;
I trampled them like mud in the streets.
You have delivered me from the attacks of
the people;
you have made me the head of nations.
People I did not know now serve me,
foreigners cower before me;
as soon as they hear of me, and they
obey me.
They all lose heart;
they come trembling from their
strongholds.
The Lord lives! Praise be to my Rock!
Exalted be God my Savior!
He is the God who avenges me,
who subdues nations under me,
who saves me from my enemies.

You exalted me above my foes;
from a violent man you rescued me.
Therefore I will praise you, Lord, among
the
Nations;
I will sing the praises of your name.
He gives his king great victories;
he shows unfailing love to his anointed,
to David and to his descendants forever.

JAH RASTAFARI PRAYER
TO REMOVE BAD LUCK

King Selassie I and Empress Mennen (Explain the bad luck happenings) I and I know you intend for me to live Joyous happy and prosperous in this life. I and I know in Rastafari there is no such thing as *bad luck*. Please give I and I the wisdom, strength and resilience to change I and I thoughts. Please help I and I to know, that what I experience on the outside is not who I and I am on the Inside. Bless I and I that I may learn your way, and know your light. In King Selassie I, and Empress Menen name, Jah Rastafari.

Burn some Frankincense and myrrh in your living room, on a Saturday morning and say the following Psalm out loud. Do this for 3 consecutive Saturdays.

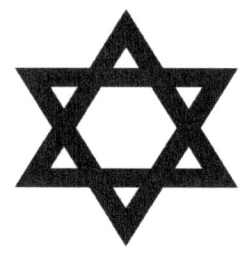

My God, my God, why have you
forsaken me?
Why are you so far from saving me,
so far from my cries of anguish?
My God, I cry out by day, but you do not
answer,
by night, but I find no rest.
Yet you are enthroned as the Holy One;
you are the one Israel praises.
In you our ancestors put their trust;
they trusted and you delivered them.
To you they cried out and were saved;
in you they trusted and were not put to
shame.
But I am a worm and not a man,
scorned by everyone, despised by the
people.
All who see me mock me;
they hurl insults, shaking their heads.

"He trusts in the Lord," they say,
"let the Lord rescue him.
Let him deliver him,
since he delights in him."
Yet you brought me out of the womb;
you made me trust in you, even at my
mother's breast.
From birth I was cast on you;
from my mother's womb you have been
my God.
Do not be far from me,
for trouble is near
and there is no one to help.
Many bulls surround me;
strong bulls of Bashan encircle me.
Roaring lions that tear their prey
open their mouths wide against me.
I am poured out like water,
and all my bones are out of joint.
My heart has turned to wax;
it has melted within me.
My mouth is dried up like a potsherd,
and my tongue sticks to the roof of my
mouth;
you lay me in the dust of death.
Dogs surround me,
a pack of villains encircles me;
they pierce my hands and my feet.

All my bones are on display;
people stare and gloat over me.
They divide my clothes among them
and cast lots for my garment.
But you, Lord, do not be far from me.
You are my strength; come quickly to
help me.
Deliver me from the sword,
my precious life from the power of the
dogs.
Rescue me from the mouth of the lions;
save me from the horns of the wild oxen.
I will declare your name to my people;
in the assembly I will praise you.
You who fear the Lord, praise him!
All you descendants of Jacob, honor him!
Revere him, all you descendants of
Israel!
For he has not despised or scorned
the suffering of the afflicted one;
he has not hidden his face from him
but has listened to his cry for help.
From you comes the theme of my praise
in the great assembly;
before those who fear you I will fulfill my
vows.
The poor will eat and be satisfied;
those who seek the Lord will praise
him—

may your hearts live forever!
All the ends of the earth
will remember and turn to the Lord,
and all the families of the nations
will bow down before him,
for dominion belongs to the Lord
and he rules over the nations.
All the rich of the earth will feast and
worship;
all who go down to the dust will kneel
before him—
those who cannot keep themselves alive.
Posterity will serve him;
future generations will be told about the
Lord.
They will proclaim his righteousness,
declaring to a people yet unborn:
He has done it!

JAH RASTAFARI PRAYER
TO BE WELL RECEIVED BY AN AUTHORITY FIGURE

(Boss, bank manager, Mother in Law etc.)

Jah you are the ruler and creator of all things. I and I, humbly ask for your help in a matter concerning a person. I ask that you shine your light over (state person's name) that they may see me and know my heart. Fill my heart with your purity, royal countenance and wisdom that I and I may be seen and heard in the most positive and loving light by (state person's name) In King Selassie I, and Empress Menen name, Jah Rastafari.

Guidebook for
Hebrew Israelite Women

Read the following Psalm 3x daily before you meet with the authority figure.

I will extol the Lord at all times;
his praise will always be on my lips.
I will glory in the Lord;
let the afflicted hear and rejoice.
Glorify the Lord with me;
let us exalt his name together.
I sought the Lord, and he answered me;
he delivered me from all my fears.
Those who look to him are radiant;
their faces are never covered with
shame.
This poor man called, and the Lord heard
him;
he saved him out of all his troubles.
The angel of the Lord encamps around
those who fear him,
and he delivers them.
Taste and see that the Lord is good;

blessed is the one who takes refuge in
him.
Fear the Lord, you his holy people,
for those who fear him lack nothing.
The lions may grow weak and hungry,
but those who seek the Lord lack no
good thing.
Come, my children, listen to me;
I will teach you the fear of the Lord.
Whoever of you loves life
and desires to see many good days,
keep your tongue from evil
and your lips from telling lies.
Turn from evil and do good;
seek peace and pursue it.
The eyes of the Lord are on the
righteous,
and his ears are attentive to their cry;
but the face of the Lord is against those
who do evil,
to blot out their name from the earth.
The righteous cry out, and the Lord hears
them;
he delivers them from all their troubles.
The Lord is close to the broken hearted
and saves those who are crushed in
spirit.
The righteous person may have many
troubles,

but the Lord delivers him from them all;
He protects all his bones,
not one of them will be broken.
Evil will slay the wicked;
the foes of the righteous will be
condemned.
The Lord will rescue his servants;
no one who takes refuge in him will be
condemned.

JAH RASTAFARI PRAYER
TO PROTECT PREGNANCIES

Dear, Empress Menen my concern is of a pregnancy. (explain why you are asking for protection of the baby) You have the Mighty hand. On my behalf please call upon Jah loving and protective angels to protect this pregnancy.

In Empress Menen name. I and I give thanks.

Read the following psalm 2x times daily till the baby is born.

Psalm 1

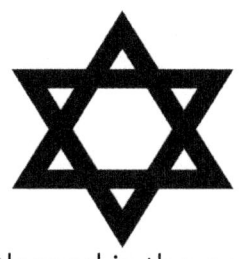

Blessed is the one
who does not walk in step with the
wicked
or stand in the way that sinners take
or sit in the company of mockers,
but whose delight is in the law of the Lord,
and who meditates on his law day and
night.
That person is like a tree planted by
streams of water,
which yields its fruit in season
and whose leaf does not wither—
whatever they do prospers.
Not so the wicked!
They are like chaff
that the wind blows away.
Therefore the wicked will not stand in
the judgment,
nor sinners in the assembly of the
righteous.
For the Lord watches over the way of
the righteous,

but the way of the wicked leads to destruction.

JAH RASTAFARI PRAYER
TO STOP GOSSIP

Jah, Babylon is a divisive, destructive and wicked place. Mankind degrades Mankind, and people use their mouth with the intent to hurt others. King Selassie I and Empress Menen, please help I and I so that gossip from _____about _____will be stopped. Your plan for my life is love, and a contented spirit. Show the Gossiper that Gossip is not of Jah, provide them with another means of expression in which they can be proud of that is not detrimental to another individual. I know you have the power to change circumstances for the better.
In King Selassie I and Empress Menen name.

Read the following Psalms until the circumstances change.

Listen to my words, Lord,
consider my lament.
Hear my cry for help,
my King and my God,
for to you I pray.
In the morning, Lord, you hear my voice;
in the morning I lay my requests before
you
and wait expectantly.
For you are not a God who is pleased with
wickedness;
with you, evil people are not welcome.
The arrogant cannot stand
in your presence.
You hate all who do wrong;
you destroy those who tell lies.
The bloodthirsty and deceitful
you, Lord, detest.

But I, by your great love,
can come into your house;
in reverence I bow down
toward your holy temple.
Lead me, Lord, in your righteousness
because of my enemies—
make your way straight before me.
Not a word from their mouth can be
trusted;
their heart is filled with malice.
Their throat is an open grave;
with their tongues they tell lies.
Declare them guilty, O God!
Let their intrigues be their downfall.
Banish them for their many sins,
for they have rebelled against you.
But let all who take refuge in you be glad;
let them ever sing for joy.
Spread your protection over them,
that those who love your name may
rejoice in you.
Surely, Lord, you bless the righteous;
you surround them with your favor as
with a shield.

JAH RASTAFARI PRAYER
TO HELP A MARRIAGE REGAIN THE LOVE

King Selassie I/Empress Mennen you are a loving couple, and Royalty of Zion. You Ruled over Ethiopia and were ascended to the Kingdom of the Most High. Please bring a healing energy to my relationship. Please bless and heal our hearts so that we may be considerate and kind towards one another. You have the mighty hand over our union.
I promise to speak highly of the power of Jah Rastafari and the things you have manifested in my life.

Say this Psalm 3x daily, to keep the relationship healthy and flowing with love and understanding.

You, Lord, showed favor to your land;
you restored the fortunes of Jacob.
You forgave the iniquity of your people
and covered all their sins.
You set aside all your wrath
and turned from your fierce anger.
Restore us again, God our Savior,
and put away your displeasure toward
us.
Will you be angry with us forever?
Will you prolong your anger through all
generations?
Will you not revive us again,
that your people may rejoice in you?
Show us your unfailing love, Lord,
and grant us your salvation.
I will listen to what God the Lord says;
he promises peace to his people, his

faithful servants—
but let them not turn to folly.
Surely his salvation is near those who fear
him,
that his glory may dwell in our land.
Love and faithfulness meet together;
righteousness and peace kiss each other.
Faithfulness springs forth from the earth,
and righteousness looks down from
heaven.
The Lord will indeed give what is good,
and our land will yield its harvest.
Righteousness goes before him
and prepares the way for his steps.

JAH RASTAFARI PRAYER
TO BRING PEACE TO THE HOME

Empress Menen and King Selassie I, please bring peace to this home. Bless this home with your Royal presence, and bless this home with your love. Fill every heart with the desire to please and serve Jah the Most High.

In King Selassie I name.

We praise you, God,
we praise you, for your Name is near;
people tell of your wonderful deeds.
You say, "I choose the appointed time;
it is I who judge with equity.
When the earth and all its people quake,
it is I who hold its pillars firm.
To the arrogant I say, 'Boast no more,'
and to the wicked, 'Do not lift up your
horns.
Do not lift your horns against heaven;
do not speak so defiantly.'"
No one from the east or the west
or from the desert can exalt themselves.
It is God who judges:
He brings one down, he exalts another.
In the hand of the Lord is a cup
full of foaming wine mixed with spices;
he pours it out, and all the wicked of the

earth
drink it down to its very dregs.
As for me, I will declare this forever;
I will sing praise to the God of Jacob,
who says, "I will cut off the horns of all
the wicked,
but the horns of the righteous will be
lifted up."

JAH RASTAFARI PRAYER
TO HEAL ADDICTIONS

Oh Jah, addiction come in all forms. Satan is very smart and has the ability to "package" temptations in a way that many of us in Babylon cannot resist.
We are addicted to other people, addicted to food, addicted to sex, addicted to the accumulation of money, etc.
King Alpha Queen Omega, please hear my heart. I find my self-addicted to _____and I ask for your powerful help to break this cycle and this addiction. Please put your strength in me, and cleanse my spirit in order that my mind body and soul may be clear of this addiction to _____.
King Selassie I, Empress Menen, I know you have the power to change circumstance for the better. I turn the

matter over to you.

In King Selassie I name.

Read the following psalm 3 x daily, until you feel you have defeated your addiction.

Lord, hear my prayer,
listen to my cry for mercy;
in your faithfulness and righteousness
come to my relief.
Do not bring your servant into judgment,
for no one living is righteous before you.
The enemy pursues me,
he crushes me to the ground;
he makes me dwell in the darkness
like those long dead.
So my spirit grows faint within me;
my heart within me is dismayed.
I remember the days of long ago;
I meditate on all your works
and consider what your hands have
done.
I spread out my hands to you;
I thirst for you like a parched land.
Answer me quickly, Lord;

my spirit fails.
Do not hide your face from me
or I will be like those who go down to
the pit.
Let the morning bring me word of your
unfailing love,
for I have put my trust in you.
Show me the way I should go,
for to you I entrust my life.
Rescue me from my enemies, Lord,
for I hide myself in you.
[1]Teach me to do your will,
for you are my God;
may your good Spirit
lead me on level ground.
For your name's sake, Lord, preserve my
life;
in your righteousness, bring me out of
trouble.
In your unfailing love, silence my
enemies;
destroy all my foes,
for I am your servant.

JAH RASTAFARI PRAYER
TO BECOME PREGNANT

King Selassie I, you are the ruler to all the
four corners of the earth. Creation is your
delight. Please help (me)
_____to become pregnant.
Make the baby healthy and provide him or
her with your Royal countenance, wisdom
and strength. Bless this baby while it is in
the womb so that he she may know you
Jah. I call for your mighty hand over this
plan. I and I give thanks.

In King Selassie I name. Jah Rastafari.

For the director of music. Of David. A
psalm.
You have searched me, Lord,
and you know me.
You know when I sit and when I rise;
you perceive my thoughts from afar.
You discern my going out and my lying
down;
you are familiar with all my ways.
Before a word is on my tongue
you, Lord, know it completely.
You hem me in behind and before,
and you lay your hand upon me.
Such knowledge is too wonderful for
me,
too lofty for me to attain.
Where can I go from your Spirit?
Where can I flee from your presence?

If I go up to the heavens, you are there;
if I make my bed in the depths, you are
there.
If I rise on the wings of the dawn,
if I settle on the far side of the sea,
even there your hand will guide me,
your right hand will hold me fast.
If I say, "Surely the darkness will hide me
and the light become night around me,"
even the darkness will not be dark to
you;
the night will shine like the day,
for darkness is as light to you.
For you created my inmost being;
you knit me together in my mother's
womb.
I praise you because I am fearfully and
wonderfully made;
your works are wonderful,
I know that full well.
My frame was not hidden from you
when I was made in the secret place,
when I was woven together in the
depths of the earth.
Your eyes saw my unformed body;
all the days ordained for me were
written in your book
before one of them came to be.
How precious to me are your thoughts,

God!
How vast is the sum of them!
were I to count them,
they would outnumber the grains of
sand—
when I awake, I am still with you.
If only you, God, would slay the wicked!
Away from me, you who are
bloodthirsty!
They speak of you with evil intent;
your adversaries misuse your name.
Do I not hate those who hate you, Lord,
and abhor those who are in rebellion
against you?
I have nothing but hatred for them;
I count them my enemies.
Search me, God, and know my heart;
test me and know my anxious thoughts.
See if there is any offensive way in me,
and lead me in the way everlasting.

JAH RASTAFARI PRAYER
TO CALM A TROUBLESOME PERSON

(such as neighbor, co-worker, tenant, roommate etc.)

Jah, as you look down from Zion you see and you know all things. You know my heart before I speak. If my heart is clean may my desire be granted. Jah, please do something to change the circumstances regarding _____so that the problem is no longer. You are the High one.

I give thanks. In King Selassie I name.

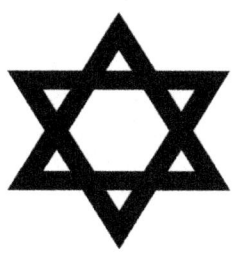

"They have greatly oppressed me from
my youth,"
let Israel say;
"they have greatly oppressed me from
my youth,
but they have not gained the victory
over me.
Plowmen have plowed my back
and made their furrows long.
But the Lord is righteous;
he has cut me free from the cords of the
wicked."
May all who hate Zion
be turned back in shame.
May they be like grass on the roof,
which withers before it can grow;
a reaper cannot fill his hands with it,

nor one who gathers fill his arms.
May those who pass by not say to them,
"The blessing of the Lord be on you;
we bless you in the name of the Lord."

JAH RASTAFARI PRAYER
TO FIND A JOB/EMPLOYMENT

Jah, Life in Babylon is not easy. I need to find work or Employment that can provide I and I with prosperity abundance, food, and shelter comfort. In Babylon bills must be paid, and food must be bought. Please help I and I to be happy and thriving in this work. In Rastafari Name. King Selassie I.

Blessed are all who fear the Lord,
who walk in obedience to him.
You will eat the fruit of your labor;
blessings and prosperity will be yours.
Your wife will be like a fruitful vine
within your house;
your children will be like olive shoots
around your table.
Yes, this will be the blessing
for the man who fears the Lord.
May the Lord bless you from Zion;
may you see the prosperity of Jerusalem
all the days of your life.
May you live to see your children's
children—
peace be on Israel.

JAH RASTAFARI PRAYER
TO HAVE VICTORY

Jah, your power is the greatest. I and I know in you I can do all things. I will carry you in my thoughts, especially at those times when I am in the presence of decision makers or in the mist of the competition.
Your power will give I and I the victory. In King Selassie I name.

Hear me, Lord, and answer me,
for I am poor and needy.
Guard my life, for I am faithful to you;
save your servant who trusts in you.
You are my God; have mercy on me,
Lord,
for I call to you all day long.
Bring joy to your servant, Lord,
for I put my trust in you.
You, Lord, are forgiving and good,
abounding in love to all who call to you.
Hear my prayer, Lord;
listen to my cry for mercy.
When I am in distress, I call to you,
because you answer me.
Among the gods there is none like you,
Lord;
no deeds can compare with yours.
9All the nations you have made
will come and worship before you, Lord;
they will bring glory to your name.
For you are great and do marvelous
deeds;
you alone are God.
Teach me your way, Lord,

that I may rely on your faithfulness;
give me an undivided heart,
that I may fear your name.
I will praise you, Lord my God, with all
my heart;
I will glorify your name forever.
For great is your love toward me;
you have delivered me from the depths,
from the realm of the dead.
Arrogant foes are attacking me, O God;
ruthless people are trying to kill me—
they have no regard for you.
But you, Lord, are a compassionate and
gracious God,
slow to anger, abounding in love and
faithfulness.
Turn to me and have mercy on me;
show your strength in behalf of your
servant;
save me, because I serve you
just as my mother did.
Give me a sign of your goodness,
that my enemies may see it and be put
to shame,
for you, Lord, have helped me and
comforted me.

JAH RASTAFARI PRAYER
TO HEAL A BROKEN HEART

Jah, my heart is broken. Something's are to last a life time, and some are to last a short while. Please place your hand over my heart. You are so highly, you have the power to heal me. Please change my thoughts so that I may remake myself, and shift my focus. I know your love for me is great. I know complete healing will come, and I know your word (King James Version Bible) is an accelerator for healing.

In King Selassie I name and Empress Menen name I and I give thanks.

Read the following Psalm early in the morning every day until you feel your heart has been fully healed.

I lift up my eyes to you,
to you who sit enthroned in heaven.
As the eyes of slaves look to the hand of
their master,
as the eyes of a female slave look to the
hand of her mistress,
so our eyes look to the Lord our God,
till he shows us his mercy.
Have mercy on us, Lord, have mercy on
us,
for we have endured no end of
contempt.
We have endured no end
of ridicule from the arrogant,
of contempt from the proud.

JAH RASTAFARI PRAYER
TO INFLUENCE THE LAW IN YOUR FAVOUR

Jah you know that Babylon likes to trick, and trap people. Please Jah keep I and I out of Babylon hands and Babylon way. Jah I and I know you intend for me to be free in your land. Please keep the Babylon law away from me and protect I and I with your laws of mercy and freedom.In King Selassie I name, Jah Rastafari.

Read the prayer every day until you feel the trouble with the law has passed.

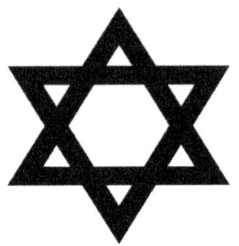

Endow the king with your justice, O God,
the royal son with your righteousness.
May he judge your people in
righteousness,
your afflicted ones with justice.
May the mountains bring prosperity to
the people,
the hills the fruit of righteousness.
May he defend the afflicted among the
people
and save the children of the needy;
may he crush the oppressor.
May he endure as long as the sun,
as long as the moon, through all
generations.
May he be like rain falling on a mown
field,
like showers watering the earth.
In his days may the righteous flourish
and prosperity abound till the moon is

no more.
May he rule from sea to sea
and from the River to the ends of the
earth.
May the desert tribes bow before him
and his enemies lick the dust.
May the kings of Tarshish and of distant
shores
bring tribute to him.
May the kings of Sheba and Seba
present him gifts.
May all kings bow down to him
and all nations serve him.
For he will deliver the needy who cry
out,
the afflicted who have no one to help.
He will take pity on the weak and the
needy
and save the needy from death.
He will rescue them from oppression
and violence,
for precious is their blood in his sight.
Long may he live!
May gold from Sheba be given him.
May people ever pray for him
and bless him all day long.
May grain abound throughout the land;
on the tops of the hills may it sway.

May the crops flourish like Lebanon
and thrive like the grass of the field.
May his name endure forever;
may it continue as long as the sun.
Then all nations will be blessed through
him,
and they will call him blessed.
Praise be to the Lord God, the God of
Israel,
who alone does marvelous deeds.
Praise be to his glorious name forever;
may the whole earth be filled with his
glory.
Amen and Amen.
This concludes the prayers of David son
of Jesse.

JAH RASTAFARI PRAYER TO PASS A TEST OR EXAM

King Selassie I, Empress Menen I and I would like your help. Please help me so that I pass the exam/test I am about to take for _____ on (state the date.) Please help me to study, understand and retain the information, and be able to apply it with ease. I know I can do this...please put your mighty hand over this.

In King Selassie I name. Jah, Rastafari.

Praise the Lord.
I will extol the Lord with all my heart
in the council of the upright and in the
assembly.
Great are the works of the Lord;
they are pondered by all who delight in
them.
Glorious and majestic are his deeds,
and his righteousness endures forever.
He has caused his wonders to be
remembered;
the Lord is gracious and compassionate.
He provides food for those who fear
him;
he remembers his covenant forever.
He has shown his people the power of
his works,
giving them the lands of other nations.
The works of his hands are faithful and
just;

all his precepts are trustworthy.
They are established for ever and ever,
enacted in faithfulness and uprightness.
He provided redemption for his people;
he ordained his covenant forever—
holy and awesome is his name.
The fear of the Lord is the beginning of
wisdom;
all who follow his precepts have good
understanding.
To him belongs eternal praise.

JAH RASTAFARI PRAYER
FOR JAH PROTECTION

Jah you are the one who created the earth and the heavens. You make the rain to fall. You make and the sun to rise and to set, you make the moon to shine at night. You are the Most Powerful, you are the Most High. Jah I ask for your protection. Keep I and I safe, and may I have no cause to feel alarm. I believe in yours your wisdom and your power. I will fast and I will continue to pray. I know you are here with me.

In King Selassie I name.

The following Psalm should be read as much as needed for the duration you need the protection.

Be sure to read the Psalm outloud.

In thee, O LORD, do I put my trust: let me never be put to confusion.

Deliver me in thy righteousness, and cause me to escape: incline thine ear unto me, and save me.

Be thou my strong habitation, whereunto I may continually resort: thou hast given commandment to save me; for thou art my rock and my fortress.

Deliver me, O my God, out of the hand of the wicked, out of the hand of the unrighteous and cruel man.

For thou art my hope, O Lord GOD: thou art my trust from my youth.

By thee have I been holden up from the womb: thou art he that took me out of my mother's bowels: my praise shall be continually of thee.

I am as a wonder unto many; but thou art my strong refuge.

Let my mouth be filled with thy praise and with thy honor all the day.

Cast me not off in the time of old age; forsake me not when my strength faileth.

For mine enemies speak against me; and they that lay wait for my soul take counsel together,

Saying, God hath forsaken him: persecute and take him; for there is none to deliver him.

O God, be not far from me: O my God, make haste for my help.

Let them be confounded and consumed that are adversaries to my soul; let them be covered with reproach and dishonor that seek my hurt.

But I will hope continually, and will yet praise thee more and more.

My mouth shall shew forth thy righteousness and thy salvation all the day; for I know not the numbers thereof.

I will go in the strength of the Lord GOD: I will make mention of thy righteousness, even of thine only.

O God, thou hast taught me from my youth: and hitherto have I declared thy wondrous works.

Now also when I am old and gray headed, O God, forsake me not; until I have shewed thy strength unto this generation, and thy power to everyone that is to come.

Thy righteousness also, O God, is very high, who hast done great things: O God, who is like unto thee!

Thou, which hast shewed me great and sore troubles, shalt quicken me again, and shalt bring me up again from the depths of the earth.

Thou shalt increase my greatness, and comfort me on every side.

I will also praise thee with the psaltery, even thy truth, O my God: unto thee will I sing with the harp, O thou Holy One of Israel.

My lips shall greatly rejoice when I sing unto thee; and my soul, which thou hast redeemed.

My tongue also shall talk of thy righteousness all the day long: for they are confounded, for they are brought unto shame, that seek my hurt.

JAH RASTAFARI PRAYER
TO BLESS A HOME

Jah, your name alone cuts and clears all negative energy. Your power, presence, and wisdom, is the highest. Please bless this home that only righteousness, love, and understanding may dwell here. Provide for us a basis of knowing, that is Royal, natural, respectful, and humble. In your name I remove any energies that do not serve you.
In King Selassie I name.

Hear my cry, O God;
listen to my prayer.
From the ends of the earth I call to you,
I call as my heart grows faint;
lead me to the rock that is higher than I.
For you have been my refuge,
a strong tower against the foe.
I long to dwell in your tent forever
and take refuge in the shelter of your
wings.
For you, God, have heard my vows;
you have given me the heritage of those
who fear your name.
Increase the days of the king's life,
his years for many generations.
May he be enthroned in God's presence
forever;
appoint your love and faithfulness to

protect him.
Then I will ever sing in praise of your name
and fulfill my vows day after day.

JAH RASTAFARI PRAYER
FOR HEALING

Jah, bring I and I close to you. Your love is the highest. I need spiritual healing and renewal. (state problem/issue) You make the sun to rise and to set, I know through you I will find spiritual Healing.
In King Selassie I name.

I will exalt you, Lord,
for you lifted me out of the depths
and did not let my enemies gloat over
me.
Lord my God, I called to you for help,
and you healed me.
You, Lord, brought me up from the realm
of the dead;
you spared me from going down to the
pit.
Sing the praises of the Lord, you his
faithful people;
praise his holy name.
For his anger lasts only a moment,
but his favor lasts a lifetime;
weeping may stay for the night,
but rejoicing comes in the morning.
When I felt secure, I said,
"I will never be shaken."
Lord, when you favored me,

you made my royal mountain stand firm;
but when you hid your face,
I was dismayed.
To you, Lord, I called;
to the Lord I cried for mercy:
"What is gained if I am silenced,
if I go down to the pit?
Will the dust praise you?
Will it proclaim your faithfulness?
Hear, Lord, and be merciful to me;
Lord, be my help."
You turned my wailing into dancing;
you removed my sackcloth and clothed
me with joy,
that my heart may sing your praises and
not be silent.
Lord my God, I will praise you forever.

JAH RASTAFARI PRAYER
TO GIVE THANKS & PRAISES

Jah, Most High, you have power over all things. I and I am grateful to you. I give you thanks, I give you thanks, I give you thanks. Yes, Jah, Rastafari.

Thanks and praises are very important in Rastafari. Builds relationship with Jah, and brings blessings.

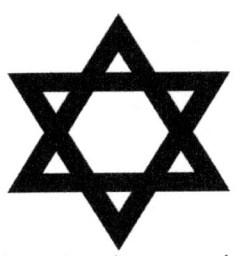

Praise the Lord.
Praise God in his sanctuary;
praise him in his mighty heavens.
Praise him for his acts of power;
praise him for his surpassing greatness.
Praise him with the sounding of the trumpet,
praise him with the harp and lyre,
praise him with timbrel and dancing,
praise him with the strings and pipe,
praise him with the clash of cymbals,
praise him with resounding cymbals.
Let everything that has breath praise the Lord.
Praise the Lord.

JAH RASTAFARI PRAYER TO END SUFFERING CAUSED BY SIN

Yes Jah, I know I suffer because I have added sin to sin. I would like to end the sin and to end the suffering. Please King Selassie I, please Empress Menen, help I and I to stop sin, and to put an end to my suffering. In Jah Rastafari name.

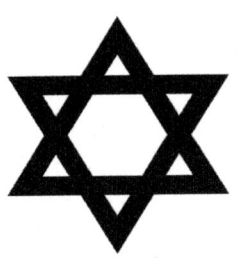

Praise the Lord, my soul;
all my inmost being, praise his holy
name.
Praise the Lord, my soul,
and forget not all his benefits—
who forgives all your sins
and heals all your diseases,
who redeems your life from the pit
and crowns you with love and
compassion,
who satisfies your desires with good things
so that your youth is renewed like the
eagle's.
The Lord works righteousness
and justice for all the oppressed.
He made known his ways to Moses,
his deeds to the people of Israel:
The Lord is compassionate and gracious,

slow to anger, abounding in love.
He will not always accuse,
nor will he harbor his anger forever;
he does not treat us as our sins deserve
or repay us according to our iniquities.
For as high as the heavens are above the earth,
so great is his love for those who fear him;
as far as the east is from the west,
so far has he removed our transgressions from us.
As a father has compassion on his children,
so the Lord has compassion on those who fear him;
for he knows how we are formed,
he remembers that we are dust.
The life of mortals is like grass,
they flourish like a flower of the field;
the wind blows over it and it is gone,
and its place remembers it no more.
But from everlasting to everlasting
the Lord's love is with those who fear him,
and his righteousness with their children's children—
with those who keep his covenant
and remember to obey his precepts.

The Lord has established his throne in
heaven,
and his kingdom rules over all.
Praise the Lord, you his angels,
you mighty ones who do his bidding,
who obey his word.
e the Lord, all his heavenly hosts,
you his servants who do his will.
Praise the Lord, all his works
everywhere in his dominion.
Praise the Lord, my soul.

Guard my life and rescue me;
do not let me be put to shame,
for I take refuge in you.
May integrity and uprightness protect me,
because my hope, Lord, is in you.
Deliver Israel, O God,
from all their troubles!

Empress Yuajah is a Toronto born Rasta. She writes, blogs and teaches the Rastafari Livity. In her spare time she spends time with her Husband and step son.
Her latest book is entitled "Blessings of Jah."
www.jamaicanrastafarianlove.com

Life as a Rasta Woman

JAH RASTAFARI PRAYERS

Empress Yuajah

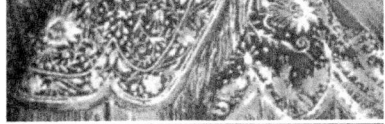

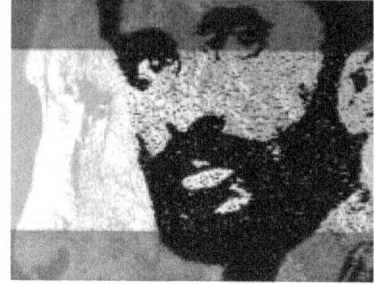

Rasta Meditation Handbook

How to Date a Jamaican Man

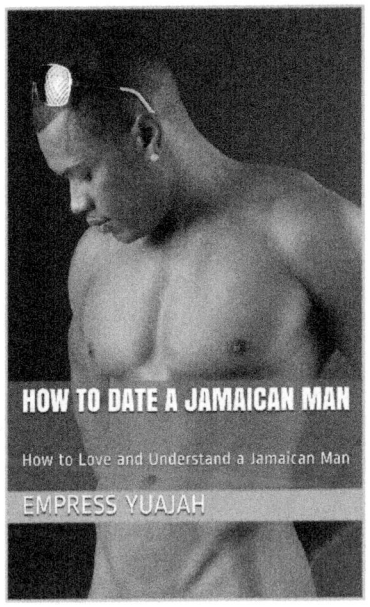

Printed in Great Britain
by Amazon

60794578R00067